The Complete Book Of Addresses

The Complete Book Of Addresses
An M&M Publications Creation.
Printed by Createspace, an Amazon.com Company.

ISBN-13: 978-1523242306
ISBN-10: 1523242302

Contacts

Contact Name: _____

_____

Telephone 1: _____
Telephone 2: _____

Mobile phone 1: _____
Mobile phone 2: _____

Fax: _____

E-mail 1: _____

_____
E-mail 2: _____

_____

Address 1: _____

_____

_____
Address 2: _____

_____

How we met: _____

_____

_____
Other details: _____

_____

_____

_____

Contact Name:_____

_____

Telephone 1:_____
Telephone 2:_____

Mobile phone 1:_____
Mobile phone 2:_____

Fax:_____

E-mail 1:_____
_____
E-mail 2:_____
_____

Address 1:_____
_____
_____
Address 2:_____
_____

How we met:_____
_____
_____
Other details:_____
_____
_____
_____

Contact Name:_____

_____

Telephone 1:_____
Telephone 2:_____

Mobile phone 1:_____
Mobile phone 2:_____

Fax:_____

E-mail 1:_____
_____

E-mail 2:_____
_____

Address 1:_____
_____

Address 2:_____
_____

How we met:_____
_____

Other details:_____
_____
_____
_____

Contact Name:_____

_____

Telephone 1:_____
Telephone 2:_____

Mobile phone 1:_____
Mobile phone 2:_____

Fax:_____

E-mail 1:_____

E-mail 2:_____

_____

Address 1:_____

_____

Address 2:_____

_____

How we met:_____

_____

Other details:_____

_____

_____

_____

Contact Name:_____

_____

Telephone 1:_____
Telephone 2:_____

Mobile phone 1:_____
Mobile phone 2:_____

Fax:_____

E-mail 1:_____

_____
E-mail 2:_____

_____

Address 1:_____

_____

_____
Address 2:_____

_____

How we met:_____

_____

_____
Other details:_____

_____

_____

_____

Contact Name:_____

_____

Telephone 1:_____
Telephone 2:_____

Mobile phone 1:_____
Mobile phone 2:_____

Fax:_____

E-mail 1:_____

_____

E-mail 2:_____

_____

Address 1:_____

_____

_____

Address 2:_____

_____

How we met:_____

_____

_____

Other details:_____

_____

_____

_____

Contact Name:_____

_____

Telephone 1:_____
Telephone 2:_____

Mobile phone 1:_____
Mobile phone 2:_____

Fax:_____

E-mail 1:_____

_____
E-mail 2:_____

_____

Address 1:_____

_____

_____
Address 2:_____

_____

How we met:_____

_____

_____
Other details:_____

_____

_____

_____

Contact Name:_____

_____

Telephone 1:_____
Telephone 2:_____

Mobile phone 1:_____
Mobile phone 2:_____

Fax:_____

E-mail 1:_____

E-mail 2:_____

_____

Address 1:_____

_____

Address 2:_____

_____

How we met:_____

_____

Other details:_____

_____

_____

_____

Contact Name: _____

_____

Telephone 1: _____
Telephone 2: _____

Mobile phone 1: _____
Mobile phone 2: _____

Fax: _____

E-mail 1: _____

_____

E-mail 2: _____

_____

Address 1: _____

_____

_____

Address 2: _____

_____

How we met: _____

_____

_____

Other details: _____

_____

_____

_____

Contact Name: _____

_____

Telephone 1: _____
Telephone 2: _____

Mobile phone 1: _____
Mobile phone 2: _____

Fax: _____

E-mail 1: _____

E-mail 2: _____

_____

Address 1: _____

_____

Address 2: _____

_____

How we met: _____

_____

Other details: _____

_____

_____

_____

Contact Name:_____

_____

Telephone 1:_____
Telephone 2:_____

Mobile phone 1:_____
Mobile phone 2:_____

Fax:_____

E-mail 1:_____

_____

E-mail 2:_____

_____

Address 1:_____

_____

_____

Address 2:_____

_____

How we met:_____

_____

_____

Other details:_____

_____

_____

_____

Contact Name: _____

_____

Telephone 1: _____
Telephone 2: _____

Mobile phone 1: _____
Mobile phone 2: _____

Fax: _____

E-mail 1: _____

_____
E-mail 2: _____

_____

Address 1: _____

_____

_____
Address 2: _____

_____

How we met: _____

_____

_____
Other details: _____

_____

_____

_____

Contact Name: _____

_____

Telephone 1: _____
Telephone 2: _____

Mobile phone 1: _____
Mobile phone 2: _____

Fax: _____

E-mail 1: _____

_____
E-mail 2: _____

_____

Address 1: _____

_____
Address 2: _____

_____

How we met: _____

_____
Other details: _____

_____
_____
_____

Contact Name:_____

_____

Telephone 1:_____
Telephone 2:_____

Mobile phone 1:_____
Mobile phone 2:_____

Fax:_____

E-mail 1:_____
_____
E-mail 2:_____
_____

Address 1:_____
_____
Address 2:_____
_____

How we met:_____
_____

Other details:_____
_____
_____
_____

Contact Name:_____

_____

Telephone 1:_____
Telephone 2:_____

Mobile phone 1:_____
Mobile phone 2:_____

Fax:_____

E-mail 1:_____

_____
E-mail 2:_____

_____

Address 1:_____

_____

Address 2:_____

_____

How we met:_____

_____

Other details:_____

_____

_____

_____

Contact Name:_____

_____

Telephone 1:_____
Telephone 2:_____

Mobile phone 1:_____
Mobile phone 2:_____

Fax:_____

E-mail 1:_____

_____
E-mail 2:_____

_____

Address 1:_____

_____

_____
Address 2:_____

_____

How we met:_____

_____

_____
Other details:_____

_____

_____

_____

Contact Name:_____

_____

Telephone 1:_____
Telephone 2:_____

Mobile phone 1:_____
Mobile phone 2:_____

Fax:_____

E-mail 1:_____

_____
E-mail 2:_____

_____

Address 1:_____

_____

_____
Address 2:_____

_____

How we met:_____

_____

_____
Other details:_____

_____

_____

_____

Contact Name:_____

_____

Telephone 1:_____
Telephone 2:_____

Mobile phone 1:_____
Mobile phone 2:_____

Fax:_____

E-mail 1:_____
_____

E-mail 2:_____
_____

Address 1:_____
_____

Address 2:_____
_____

How we met:_____
_____

Other details:_____
_____
_____
_____

Contact Name: _____

_____

Telephone 1: _____
Telephone 2: _____

Mobile phone 1: _____
Mobile phone 2: _____

Fax: _____

E-mail 1: _____

_____
E-mail 2: _____

_____

Address 1: _____

_____

_____
Address 2: _____

_____

How we met: _____

_____

_____
Other details: _____

_____

_____

_____

Contact Name: _____

_____

Telephone 1: _____
Telephone 2: _____

Mobile phone 1: _____
Mobile phone 2: _____

Fax: _____

E-mail 1: _____

_____
E-mail 2: _____

_____

Address 1: _____

_____

_____
Address 2: _____

_____

How we met: _____

_____

_____
Other details: _____

_____

_____

_____

Contact Name: _____

_____

Telephone 1: _____
Telephone 2: _____

Mobile phone 1: _____
Mobile phone 2: _____

Fax: _____

E-mail 1: _____

_____

E-mail 2: _____

_____

Address 1: _____

_____

Address 2: _____

_____

How we met: _____

_____

Other details: _____

_____

_____

_____

Contact Name: _____

_____

Telephone 1: _____
Telephone 2: _____

Mobile phone 1: _____
Mobile phone 2: _____

Fax: _____

E-mail 1: _____

_____
E-mail 2: _____

_____

Address 1: _____

_____
Address 2: _____

_____

How we met: _____

_____
Other details: _____

_____

_____

_____

Contact Name:_____

_____

Telephone 1:_____
Telephone 2:_____

Mobile phone 1:_____
Mobile phone 2:_____

Fax:_____

E-mail 1:_____

_____

E-mail 2:_____

_____

Address 1:_____

_____

_____

Address 2:_____

_____

How we met:_____

_____

_____

Other details:_____

_____

_____

_____

Contact Name:_____

_____

Telephone 1:_____
Telephone 2:_____

Mobile phone 1:_____
Mobile phone 2:_____

Fax:_____

E-mail 1:_____

_____

E-mail 2:_____

_____

Address 1:_____

_____

_____

Address 2:_____

_____

How we met:_____

_____

_____

Other details:_____

_____

_____

_____

Contact Name: _____

_____

Telephone 1: _____
Telephone 2: _____

Mobile phone 1: _____
Mobile phone 2: _____

Fax: _____

E-mail 1: _____

_____

E-mail 2: _____

_____

Address 1: _____

_____

Address 2: _____

_____

How we met: _____

_____

Other details: _____

_____

_____

_____

Contact Name: _____

_____

Telephone 1: _____
Telephone 2: _____

Mobile phone 1: _____
Mobile phone 2: _____

Fax: _____

E-mail 1: _____

E-mail 2: _____

_____

Address 1: _____

_____

Address 2: _____

_____

How we met: _____

_____

Other details: _____

_____

_____

_____

Contact Name:_____

_____

Telephone 1:_____
Telephone 2:_____

Mobile phone 1:_____
Mobile phone 2:_____

Fax:_____

E-mail 1:_____
_____

E-mail 2:_____
_____

Address 1:_____
_____
_____

Address 2:_____
_____

How we met:_____
_____
_____

Other details:_____
_____
_____
_____

Contact Name: _____

_____

Telephone 1: _____
Telephone 2: _____

Mobile phone 1: _____
Mobile phone 2: _____

Fax: _____

E-mail 1: _____
_____
E-mail 2: _____
_____

Address 1: _____
_____
Address 2: _____
_____

How we met: _____
_____
Other details: _____
_____
_____
_____

Contact Name:_____

_____

Telephone 1:_____
Telephone 2:_____

Mobile phone 1:_____
Mobile phone 2:_____

Fax:_____

E-mail 1:_____

_____

E-mail 2:_____

_____

Address 1:_____

_____

_____

Address 2:_____

_____

How we met:_____

_____

_____

Other details:_____

_____

_____

_____

Contact Name:_____

_____

Telephone 1:_____
Telephone 2:_____

Mobile phone 1:_____
Mobile phone 2:_____

Fax:_____

E-mail 1:_____

_____
E-mail 2:_____

_____

Address 1:_____

_____

Address 2:_____

_____

How we met:_____

_____

Other details:_____

_____

_____

_____

Contact Name:_____

_____

Telephone 1:_____
Telephone 2:_____

Mobile phone 1:_____
Mobile phone 2:_____

Fax:_____

E-mail 1:_____

_____
E-mail 2:_____

_____

Address 1:_____

_____

_____
Address 2:_____

_____

How we met:_____

_____

_____
Other details:_____

_____

_____

_____

Contact Name: _____

_____

Telephone 1: _____
Telephone 2: _____

Mobile phone 1: _____
Mobile phone 2: _____

Fax: _____

E-mail 1: _____
_____
E-mail 2: _____
_____

Address 1: _____
_____
Address 2: _____
_____

How we met: _____
_____
Other details: _____
_____
_____
_____

Contact Name: _____

_____

Telephone 1: _____
Telephone 2: _____

Mobile phone 1: _____
Mobile phone 2: _____

Fax: _____

E-mail 1: _____

_____

E-mail 2: _____

_____

Address 1: _____

_____

_____

Address 2: _____

_____

How we met: _____

_____

_____

Other details: _____

_____

_____

_____

Contact Name:_____

_____

Telephone 1:_____
Telephone 2:_____

Mobile phone 1:_____
Mobile phone 2:_____

Fax:_____

E-mail 1:_____

_____
E-mail 2:_____

_____

Address 1:_____

_____

_____
Address 2:_____

_____

How we met:_____

_____

_____
Other details:_____

_____

_____

_____

Contact Name:_____

_____

Telephone 1:_____
Telephone 2:_____

Mobile phone 1:_____
Mobile phone 2:_____

Fax:_____

E-mail 1:_____
_____

E-mail 2:_____
_____

Address 1:_____
_____
_____

Address 2:_____
_____

How we met:_____
_____
_____

Other details:_____
_____
_____
_____

Contact Name:_____

_____

Telephone 1:_____
Telephone 2:_____

Mobile phone 1:_____
Mobile phone 2:_____

Fax:_____

E-mail 1:_____

_____
E-mail 2:_____

_____

Address 1:_____

_____

_____
Address 2:_____

_____

How we met:_____

_____

_____
Other details:_____

_____

_____

_____

Contact Name: _____

_____

Telephone 1: _____
Telephone 2: _____

Mobile phone 1: _____
Mobile phone 2: _____

Fax: _____

E-mail 1: _____

_____
E-mail 2: _____

_____

Address 1: _____

_____

_____
Address 2: _____

_____

How we met: _____

_____

_____
Other details: _____

_____

_____

_____

Contact Name: _____

_____

Telephone 1: _____
Telephone 2: _____

Mobile phone 1: _____
Mobile phone 2: _____

Fax: _____

E-mail 1: _____

_____
E-mail 2: _____

_____

Address 1: _____

_____

_____
Address 2: _____

_____

How we met: _____

_____

_____
Other details: _____

_____

_____

_____

Contact Name:_____

_____

Telephone 1:_____
Telephone 2:_____

Mobile phone 1:_____
Mobile phone 2:_____

Fax:_____

E-mail 1:_____

_____

E-mail 2:_____

_____

Address 1:_____

_____

Address 2:_____

_____

How we met:_____

_____

Other details:_____

_____

_____

_____

Contact Name: _____

_____

Telephone 1: _____
Telephone 2: _____

Mobile phone 1: _____
Mobile phone 2: _____

Fax: _____

E-mail 1: _____

E-mail 2: _____

_____

Address 1: _____

_____

Address 2: _____

_____

How we met: _____

_____

Other details: _____

_____

_____

_____

Contact Name: _____

_____

Telephone 1: _____
Telephone 2: _____

Mobile phone 1: _____
Mobile phone 2: _____

Fax: _____

E-mail 1: _____

_____

E-mail 2: _____

_____

Address 1: _____

_____

Address 2: _____

_____

How we met: _____

_____

Other details: _____

_____

_____

_____

Contact Name: _____

_____

Telephone 1: _____
Telephone 2: _____

Mobile phone 1: _____
Mobile phone 2: _____

Fax: _____

E-mail 1: _____
_____
E-mail 2: _____
_____

Address 1: _____
_____
_____
Address 2: _____
_____

How we met: _____
_____
_____
Other details: _____
_____
_____
_____

Contact Name: _____

_____

Telephone 1:_____
Telephone 2:_____

Mobile phone 1:_____
Mobile phone 2:_____

Fax:_____

E-mail 1:_____

_____
E-mail 2:_____

_____

Address 1:_____

_____

_____
Address 2:_____

_____

How we met:_____

_____

_____
Other details:_____

_____

_____

_____

Contact Name:_____

_____

Telephone 1:_____
Telephone 2:_____

Mobile phone 1:_____
Mobile phone 2:_____

Fax:_____

E-mail 1:_____

E-mail 2:_____

Address 1:_____

_____

Address 2:_____

_____

How we met:_____

_____

Other details:_____

_____

_____

_____

Contact Name:_____

_____

Telephone 1:_____
Telephone 2:_____

Mobile phone 1:_____
Mobile phone 2:_____

Fax:_____

E-mail 1:_____

_____
E-mail 2:_____

_____

Address 1:_____

_____

_____
Address 2:_____

_____

How we met:_____

_____

_____
Other details:_____

_____

_____

_____

Contact Name:_____

_____

Telephone 1:_____
Telephone 2:_____

Mobile phone 1:_____
Mobile phone 2:_____

Fax:_____

E-mail 1:_____

_____
E-mail 2:_____

_____

Address 1:_____

_____

Address 2:_____

_____

How we met:_____

_____

Other details:_____

_____
_____
_____

Contact Name:_____

_____

Telephone 1:_____
Telephone 2:_____

Mobile phone 1:_____
Mobile phone 2:_____

Fax:_____

E-mail 1:_____

_____
E-mail 2:_____

_____

Address 1:_____

_____

Address 2:_____

_____

How we met:_____

_____

Other details:_____

_____

_____

_____

Contact Name: _____

_____

Telephone 1: _____
Telephone 2: _____

Mobile phone 1: _____
Mobile phone 2: _____

Fax: _____

E-mail 1: _____
_____

E-mail 2: _____
_____

Address 1: _____
_____
_____

Address 2: _____
_____

How we met: _____
_____

Other details: _____
_____
_____
_____

Contact Name: _____

_____

Telephone 1: _____
Telephone 2: _____

Mobile phone 1: _____
Mobile phone 2: _____

Fax: _____

E-mail 1: _____

_____
E-mail 2: _____

_____

Address 1: _____

_____
_____
Address 2: _____

_____

How we met: _____

_____
_____
Other details: _____

_____
_____
_____

Contact Name:_____

_____

Telephone 1:_____
Telephone 2:_____

Mobile phone 1:_____
Mobile phone 2:_____

Fax:_____

E-mail 1:_____

_____
E-mail 2:_____

_____

Address 1:_____

_____

_____
Address 2:_____

_____

How we met:_____

_____

_____
Other details:_____

_____

_____

_____

Contact Name: _____

_____

Telephone 1: _____
Telephone 2: _____

Mobile phone 1: _____
Mobile phone 2: _____

Fax: _____

E-mail 1: _____

_____
E-mail 2: _____

_____

Address 1: _____

_____

_____
Address 2: _____

_____

How we met: _____

_____

_____
Other details: _____

_____

_____

_____

Contact Name:_____

_____

Telephone 1:_____
Telephone 2:_____

Mobile phone 1:_____
Mobile phone 2:_____

Fax:_____

E-mail 1:_____

E-mail 2:_____

_____

Address 1:_____

_____

Address 2:_____

_____

How we met:_____

_____

Other details:_____

_____

_____

_____

Contact Name: _____

_____

Telephone 1: _____
Telephone 2: _____

Mobile phone 1: _____
Mobile phone 2: _____

Fax: _____

E-mail 1: _____

_____

E-mail 2: _____

_____

Address 1: _____

_____

_____

Address 2: _____

_____

How we met: _____

_____

_____

Other details: _____

_____

_____

_____

Contact Name:_____

_____

Telephone 1:_____
Telephone 2:_____

Mobile phone 1:_____
Mobile phone 2:_____

Fax:_____

E-mail 1:_____

E-mail 2:_____

_____

Address 1:_____

_____

Address 2:_____

_____

How we met:_____

_____

Other details:_____

_____

_____

_____

Contact Name:_____

_____

Telephone 1:_____
Telephone 2:_____

Mobile phone 1:_____
Mobile phone 2:_____

Fax:_____

E-mail 1:_____

_____
E-mail 2:_____

_____

Address 1:_____

_____

_____
Address 2:_____

_____

How we met:_____

_____

_____
Other details:_____

_____

_____

_____

Contact Name:_____

_____

Telephone 1:_____
Telephone 2:_____

Mobile phone 1:_____
Mobile phone 2:_____

Fax:_____

E-mail 1:_____

E-mail 2:_____

_____

Address 1:_____

_____

Address 2:_____

_____

How we met:_____

_____

Other details:_____

_____

_____

_____

Contact Name:_____

_____

Telephone 1:_____
Telephone 2:_____

Mobile phone 1:_____
Mobile phone 2:_____

Fax:_____

E-mail 1:_____
_____
E-mail 2:_____
_____

Address 1:_____
_____
_____
Address 2:_____
_____

How we met:_____
_____
_____
Other details:_____
_____
_____
_____

Contact Name:_____

_____

Telephone 1:_____
Telephone 2:_____

Mobile phone 1:_____
Mobile phone 2:_____

Fax:_____

E-mail 1:_____
_____
E-mail 2:_____
_____

Address 1:_____
_____
Address 2:_____
_____

How we met:_____
_____
Other details:_____
_____
_____
_____

Contact Name: _____

_____

Telephone 1: _____
Telephone 2: _____

Mobile phone 1: _____
Mobile phone 2: _____

Fax: _____

E-mail 1: _____

_____

E-mail 2: _____

_____

Address 1: _____

_____

_____

Address 2: _____

_____

How we met: _____

_____

_____

Other details: _____

_____

_____

_____

Contact Name: _____

_____

Telephone 1: _____
Telephone 2: _____

Mobile phone 1: _____
Mobile phone 2: _____

Fax: _____

E-mail 1: _____

_____

E-mail 2: _____

_____

Address 1: _____

_____

_____

Address 2: _____

_____

How we met: _____

_____

_____

Other details: _____

_____

_____

_____

Contact Name: _____

_____

Telephone 1: _____
Telephone 2: _____

Mobile phone 1: _____
Mobile phone 2: _____

Fax: _____

E-mail 1: _____

_____

E-mail 2: _____

_____

Address 1: _____

_____

Address 2: _____

_____

How we met: _____

_____

Other details: _____

_____

_____

_____

Contact Name:_____

_____

Telephone 1:_____
Telephone 2:_____

Mobile phone 1:_____
Mobile phone 2:_____

Fax:_____

E-mail 1:_____

E-mail 2:_____

_____

Address 1:_____

_____

Address 2:_____

_____

How we met:_____

_____

Other details:_____

_____

_____

_____

Contact Name:_____

_____

Telephone 1:_____
Telephone 2:_____

Mobile phone 1:_____
Mobile phone 2:_____

Fax:_____

E-mail 1:_____

_____

E-mail 2:_____

_____

Address 1:_____

_____

_____

Address 2:_____

_____

How we met:_____

_____

_____

Other details:_____

_____

_____

_____

Contact Name:_____

_____

Telephone 1:_____
Telephone 2:_____

Mobile phone 1:_____
Mobile phone 2:_____

Fax:_____

E-mail 1:_____
_____
E-mail 2:_____
_____

Address 1:_____
_____
Address 2:_____
_____

How we met:_____
_____
Other details:_____
_____
_____
_____

Contact Name:_____

_____

Telephone 1:_____
Telephone 2:_____

Mobile phone 1:_____
Mobile phone 2:_____

Fax:_____

E-mail 1:_____

_____

E-mail 2:_____

_____

Address 1:_____

_____

_____

Address 2:_____

_____

How we met:_____

_____

_____

Other details:_____

_____

_____

_____

Contact Name:_____

_____

Telephone 1:_____
Telephone 2:_____

Mobile phone 1:_____
Mobile phone 2:_____

Fax:_____

E-mail 1:_____
_____
E-mail 2:_____
_____

Address 1:_____
_____
_____
Address 2:_____
_____

How we met:_____
_____
_____
Other details:_____
_____
_____
_____

Contact Name: _____

_____

Telephone 1: _____
Telephone 2: _____

Mobile phone 1: _____
Mobile phone 2: _____

Fax: _____

E-mail 1: _____

_____

E-mail 2: _____

_____

Address 1: _____

_____

_____

Address 2: _____

_____

How we met: _____

_____

_____

Other details: _____

_____

_____

_____

Contact Name:_____

_____

Telephone 1:_____
Telephone 2:_____

Mobile phone 1:_____
Mobile phone 2:_____

Fax:_____

E-mail 1:_____
_____
E-mail 2:_____
_____

Address 1:_____
_____
Address 2:_____
_____

How we met:_____
_____
Other details:_____
_____
_____
_____

Contact Name:_____

_____

Telephone 1:_____
Telephone 2:_____

Mobile phone 1:_____
Mobile phone 2:_____

Fax:_____

E-mail 1:_____

_____

E-mail 2:_____

_____

Address 1:_____

_____

_____

Address 2:_____

_____

How we met:_____

_____

_____

Other details:_____

_____

_____

_____

Contact Name:_____

_____

Telephone 1:_____
Telephone 2:_____

Mobile phone 1:_____
Mobile phone 2:_____

Fax:_____

E-mail 1:_____
_____
E-mail 2:_____
_____

Address 1:_____
_____
_____
Address 2:_____
_____

How we met:_____
_____
_____
Other details:_____
_____
_____
_____

Contact Name:_____

_____

Telephone 1:_____
Telephone 2:_____

Mobile phone 1:_____
Mobile phone 2:_____

Fax:_____

E-mail 1:_____

_____

E-mail 2:_____

_____

Address 1:_____

_____

_____

Address 2:_____

_____

How we met:_____

_____

_____

Other details:_____

_____

_____

_____

Contact Name:_____

_____

Telephone 1:_____
Telephone 2:_____

Mobile phone 1:_____
Mobile phone 2:_____

Fax:_____

E-mail 1:_____
_____
E-mail 2:_____
_____

Address 1:_____
_____
_____
Address 2:_____
_____

How we met:_____
_____
_____
Other details:_____
_____
_____
_____

Contact Name: _____

_____

Telephone 1: _____
Telephone 2: _____

Mobile phone 1: _____
Mobile phone 2: _____

Fax: _____

E-mail 1: _____

_____
E-mail 2: _____

_____

Address 1: _____

_____

_____
Address 2: _____

_____

How we met: _____

_____

_____
Other details: _____

_____

_____

_____

Contact Name:_____

_____

Telephone 1:_____
Telephone 2:_____

Mobile phone 1:_____
Mobile phone 2:_____

Fax:_____

E-mail 1:_____

E-mail 2:_____

_____

Address 1:_____

_____

Address 2:_____

_____

How we met:_____

_____

Other details:_____

_____

_____

_____

Contact Name: _____

_____

Telephone 1: _____
Telephone 2: _____

Mobile phone 1: _____
Mobile phone 2: _____

Fax: _____

E-mail 1: _____

_____

E-mail 2: _____

_____

Address 1: _____

_____

_____

Address 2: _____

_____

How we met: _____

_____

_____

Other details: _____

_____

_____

_____

Contact Name:_____

_____

Telephone 1:_____
Telephone 2:_____

Mobile phone 1:_____
Mobile phone 2:_____

Fax:_____

E-mail 1:_____

E-mail 2:_____

_____

Address 1:_____

_____

Address 2:_____

_____

How we met:_____

_____

Other details:_____

_____

_____

_____

Contact Name:_____

_____

Telephone 1:_____
Telephone 2:_____

Mobile phone 1:_____
Mobile phone 2:_____

Fax:_____

E-mail 1:_____

_____

E-mail 2:_____

_____

Address 1:_____

_____

_____

Address 2:_____

_____

How we met:_____

_____

_____

Other details:_____

_____

_____

_____

Contact Name:_____

_____

Telephone 1:_____
Telephone 2:_____

Mobile phone 1:_____
Mobile phone 2:_____

Fax:_____

E-mail 1:_____

E-mail 2:_____

_____

Address 1:_____

_____

Address 2:_____

_____

How we met:_____

_____

Other details:_____

_____

_____

_____

Contact Name:_____

_____

Telephone 1:_____
Telephone 2:_____

Mobile phone 1:_____
Mobile phone 2:_____

Fax:_____

E-mail 1:_____

_____

E-mail 2:_____

_____

Address 1:_____

_____

_____

Address 2:_____

_____

How we met:_____

_____

_____

Other details:_____

_____

_____

_____

Contact Name:_____

_____

Telephone 1:_____
Telephone 2:_____

Mobile phone 1:_____
Mobile phone 2:_____

Fax:_____

E-mail 1:_____

E-mail 2:_____

_____

Address 1:_____

_____

Address 2:_____

_____

How we met:_____

_____

Other details:_____

_____

_____

_____

Contact Name:_____

_____

Telephone 1:_____
Telephone 2:_____

Mobile phone 1:_____
Mobile phone 2:_____

Fax:_____

E-mail 1:_____

_____

E-mail 2:_____

_____

Address 1:_____

_____

Address 2:_____

_____

How we met:_____

_____

Other details:_____

_____

_____

_____

Contact Name:_____

_____

Telephone 1:_____
Telephone 2:_____

Mobile phone 1:_____
Mobile phone 2:_____

Fax:_____

E-mail 1:_____

_____
E-mail 2:_____

_____

Address 1:_____

_____

Address 2:_____

_____

How we met:_____

_____

Other details:_____

_____

_____

_____

Contact Name: _____

_____

Telephone 1: _____
Telephone 2: _____

Mobile phone 1: _____
Mobile phone 2: _____

Fax: _____

E-mail 1: _____

_____

E-mail 2: _____

_____

Address 1: _____

_____

Address 2: _____

_____

How we met: _____

_____

Other details: _____

_____

_____

_____

Contact Name:_____

_____

Telephone 1:_____
Telephone 2:_____

Mobile phone 1:_____
Mobile phone 2:_____

Fax:_____

E-mail 1:_____

_____
E-mail 2:_____

_____

Address 1:_____

_____

Address 2:_____

_____

How we met:_____

_____

Other details:_____

_____

_____

_____

Contact Name: _____

_____

Telephone 1: _____
Telephone 2: _____

Mobile phone 1: _____
Mobile phone 2: _____

Fax: _____

E-mail 1: _____

_____
E-mail 2: _____

_____

Address 1: _____

_____

_____
Address 2: _____

_____

How we met: _____

_____

_____
Other details: _____

_____

_____

_____

Contact Name:_____

_____

Telephone 1:_____
Telephone 2:_____

Mobile phone 1:_____
Mobile phone 2:_____

Fax:_____

E-mail 1:_____

E-mail 2:_____

_____

Address 1:_____

_____

Address 2:_____

_____

How we met:_____

_____

Other details:_____

_____

_____

_____

Contact Name:_____

_____

Telephone 1:_____
Telephone 2:_____

Mobile phone 1:_____
Mobile phone 2:_____

Fax:_____

E-mail 1:_____

_____

E-mail 2:_____

_____

Address 1:_____

_____

Address 2:_____

_____

How we met:_____

_____

Other details:_____

_____

_____

_____

Contact Name:_____

_____

Telephone 1:_____
Telephone 2:_____

Mobile phone 1:_____
Mobile phone 2:_____

Fax:_____

E-mail 1:_____

_____
E-mail 2:_____

_____

Address 1:_____

_____

_____
Address 2:_____

_____

How we met:_____

_____

_____
Other details:_____

_____

_____

_____

Contact Name:_____

_____

Telephone 1:_____
Telephone 2:_____

Mobile phone 1:_____
Mobile phone 2:_____

Fax:_____

E-mail 1:_____

_____

E-mail 2:_____

_____

Address 1:_____

_____

_____

Address 2:_____

_____

How we met:_____

_____

_____

Other details:_____

_____

_____

_____

Contact Name:_____

_____

Telephone 1:_____
Telephone 2:_____

Mobile phone 1:_____
Mobile phone 2:_____

Fax:_____

E-mail 1:_____
_____
E-mail 2:_____
_____

Address 1:_____
_____
Address 2:_____
_____

How we met:_____
_____
Other details:_____
_____
_____
_____

Contact Name:_____

_____

Telephone 1:_____
Telephone 2:_____

Mobile phone 1:_____
Mobile phone 2:_____

Fax:_____

E-mail 1:_____

_____

E-mail 2:_____

_____

Address 1:_____

_____

Address 2:_____

_____

How we met:_____

_____

Other details:_____

_____

_____

Contact Name:_____

_____

Telephone 1:_____
Telephone 2:_____

Mobile phone 1:_____
Mobile phone 2:_____

Fax:_____

E-mail 1:_____

_____

E-mail 2:_____

_____

Address 1:_____

_____

_____

Address 2:_____

_____

How we met:_____

_____

_____

Other details:_____

_____

_____

_____

Contact Name: _____

_____

Telephone 1: _____
Telephone 2: _____

Mobile phone 1: _____
Mobile phone 2: _____

Fax: _____

E-mail 1: _____

_____

E-mail 2: _____

_____

Address 1: _____

_____

_____

Address 2: _____

_____

How we met: _____

_____

_____

Other details: _____

_____

_____

_____

Contact Name:_____

_____

Telephone 1:_____
Telephone 2:_____

Mobile phone 1:_____
Mobile phone 2:_____

Fax:_____

E-mail 1:_____

E-mail 2:_____

_____

Address 1:_____

_____

Address 2:_____

_____

How we met:_____

_____

Other details:_____

_____

_____

_____

Contact Name: _____

_____

Telephone 1: _____
Telephone 2: _____

Mobile phone 1: _____
Mobile phone 2: _____

Fax: _____

E-mail 1: _____

_____

E-mail 2: _____

_____

Address 1: _____

_____

_____

Address 2: _____

_____

How we met: _____

_____

_____

Other details: _____

_____

_____

_____

Contact Name: _____

_____

Telephone 1: _____
Telephone 2: _____

Mobile phone 1: _____
Mobile phone 2: _____

Fax: _____

E-mail 1: _____

E-mail 2: _____

_____

Address 1: _____

_____

Address 2: _____

_____

How we met: _____

_____

Other details: _____

_____

_____

_____

Contact Name:_____

_____

Telephone 1:_____
Telephone 2:_____

Mobile phone 1:_____
Mobile phone 2:_____

Fax:_____

E-mail 1:_____

_____

E-mail 2:_____

_____

Address 1:_____

_____

_____

Address 2:_____

_____

How we met:_____

_____

_____

Other details:_____

_____

_____

_____

Contact Name: _____

_____

Telephone 1: _____
Telephone 2: _____

Mobile phone 1: _____
Mobile phone 2: _____

Fax: _____

E-mail 1: _____
_____
E-mail 2: _____
_____

Address 1: _____
_____
_____
Address 2: _____
_____

How we met: _____
_____
_____
Other details: _____
_____
_____
_____

Contact Name:_____

_____

Telephone 1:_____
Telephone 2:_____

Mobile phone 1:_____
Mobile phone 2:_____

Fax:_____

E-mail 1:_____

_____

E-mail 2:_____

_____

Address 1:_____

_____

Address 2:_____

_____

How we met:_____

_____

Other details:_____

_____

_____

_____

Contact Name:_____

_____

Telephone 1:_____
Telephone 2:_____

Mobile phone 1:_____
Mobile phone 2:_____

Fax:_____

E-mail 1:_____
_____

E-mail 2:_____
_____

Address 1:_____
_____

Address 2:_____
_____

How we met:_____
_____

Other details:_____
_____
_____
_____

Contact Name:_____

_____

Telephone 1:_____
Telephone 2:_____

Mobile phone 1:_____
Mobile phone 2:_____

Fax:_____

E-mail 1:_____

_____

E-mail 2:_____

_____

Address 1:_____

_____

Address 2:_____

_____

How we met:_____

_____

Other details:_____

_____

_____

_____

Contact Name: _____

_____

Telephone 1: _____
Telephone 2: _____

Mobile phone 1: _____
Mobile phone 2: _____

Fax: _____

E-mail 1: _____

E-mail 2: _____

Address 1: _____

Address 2: _____

How we met: _____

Other details: _____

Contact Name:_____

_____

Telephone 1:_____
Telephone 2:_____

Mobile phone 1:_____
Mobile phone 2:_____

Fax:_____

E-mail 1:_____

_____
E-mail 2:_____

_____

Address 1:_____

_____
Address 2:_____

_____

How we met:_____

_____
Other details:_____

_____

_____

_____

Contact Name:_____

_____

Telephone 1:_____
Telephone 2:_____

Mobile phone 1:_____
Mobile phone 2:_____

Fax:_____

E-mail 1:_____

E-mail 2:_____

_____

Address 1:_____

_____

Address 2:_____

_____

How we met:_____

_____

Other details:_____

_____

_____

_____

Contact Name:_____
_____

Telephone 1:_____
Telephone 2:_____

Mobile phone 1:_____
Mobile phone 2:_____

Fax:_____

E-mail 1:_____
_____
E-mail 2:_____
_____

Address 1:_____
_____
Address 2:_____
_____

How we met:_____
_____
Other details:_____
_____
_____
_____

Contact Name:_____

_____

Telephone 1:_____
Telephone 2:_____

Mobile phone 1:_____
Mobile phone 2:_____

Fax:_____

E-mail 1:_____
_____
E-mail 2:_____
_____

Address 1:_____
_____
_____
Address 2:_____
_____

How we met:_____
_____
_____
Other details:_____
_____
_____
_____

Contact Name: _____

_____

Telephone 1: _____
Telephone 2: _____

Mobile phone 1: _____
Mobile phone 2: _____

Fax: _____

E-mail 1: _____

_____

E-mail 2: _____

_____

Address 1: _____

_____

_____

Address 2: _____

_____

How we met: _____

_____

_____

Other details: _____

_____

_____

_____

Contact Name:_____

_____

Telephone 1:_____
Telephone 2:_____

Mobile phone 1:_____
Mobile phone 2:_____

Fax:_____

E-mail 1:_____

_____
E-mail 2:_____

_____

Address 1:_____

_____

Address 2:_____

_____

How we met:_____

_____

Other details:_____

_____

_____

_____

Contact Name:_____

_____

Telephone 1:_____
Telephone 2:_____

Mobile phone 1:_____
Mobile phone 2:_____

Fax:_____

E-mail 1:_____
_____
E-mail 2:_____
_____

Address 1:_____
_____
_____
Address 2:_____
_____

How we met:_____
_____
_____
Other details:_____
_____
_____
_____

Contact Name:_____

_____

Telephone 1:_____
Telephone 2:_____

Mobile phone 1:_____
Mobile phone 2:_____

Fax:_____

E-mail 1:_____
_____
E-mail 2:_____
_____

Address 1:_____
_____
_____
Address 2:_____
_____

How we met:_____
_____
_____
Other details:_____
_____
_____
_____

Contact Name:_____

_____

Telephone 1:_____
Telephone 2:_____

Mobile phone 1:_____
Mobile phone 2:_____

Fax:_____

E-mail 1:_____

_____

E-mail 2:_____

_____

Address 1:_____

_____

Address 2:_____

_____

How we met:_____

_____

Other details:_____

_____

_____

_____

Contact Name: _____

_____

Telephone 1: _____
Telephone 2: _____

Mobile phone 1: _____
Mobile phone 2: _____

Fax: _____

E-mail 1: _____

_____
E-mail 2: _____

_____

Address 1: _____

_____

_____
Address 2: _____

_____

How we met: _____

_____

_____
Other details: _____

_____

_____

_____

Contact Name: _____

_____

Telephone 1: _____
Telephone 2: _____

Mobile phone 1: _____
Mobile phone 2: _____

Fax: _____

E-mail 1: _____

_____
E-mail 2: _____

_____

Address 1: _____

_____
_____
Address 2: _____

_____

How we met: _____

_____
_____
Other details: _____

_____
_____
_____

Contact Name:_____

_____

Telephone 1:_____
Telephone 2:_____

Mobile phone 1:_____
Mobile phone 2:_____

Fax:_____

E-mail 1:_____

_____
E-mail 2:_____

_____

Address 1:_____

_____

Address 2:_____

_____

How we met:_____

_____

Other details:_____

_____

_____

_____

Contact Name:_____

_____

Telephone 1:_____
Telephone 2:_____

Mobile phone 1:_____
Mobile phone 2:_____

Fax:_____

E-mail 1:_____

_____

E-mail 2:_____

_____

Address 1:_____

_____

Address 2:_____

_____

How we met:_____

_____

Other details:_____

_____

_____

_____

Contact Name: _____

_____

Telephone 1: _____
Telephone 2: _____

Mobile phone 1: _____
Mobile phone 2: _____

Fax: _____

E-mail 1: _____
_____
E-mail 2: _____
_____

Address 1: _____
_____
Address 2: _____
_____

How we met: _____
_____
Other details: _____
_____
_____
_____

Contact Name:_____

_____

Telephone 1:_____
Telephone 2:_____

Mobile phone 1:_____
Mobile phone 2:_____

Fax:_____

E-mail 1:_____

_____
E-mail 2:_____

_____

Address 1:_____

_____
Address 2:_____

_____

How we met:_____

_____
Other details:_____

_____
_____
_____

Contact Name: _____

_____

Telephone 1: _____
Telephone 2: _____

Mobile phone 1: _____
Mobile phone 2: _____

Fax: _____

E-mail 1: _____
_____

E-mail 2: _____
_____

Address 1: _____
_____

Address 2: _____
_____

How we met: _____
_____

Other details: _____
_____
_____
_____

Contact Name: _____

_____

Telephone 1: _____
Telephone 2: _____

Mobile phone 1: _____
Mobile phone 2: _____

Fax: _____

E-mail 1: _____

_____
E-mail 2: _____

_____

Address 1: _____

_____

_____
Address 2: _____

_____

How we met: _____

_____

_____
Other details: _____

_____

_____

_____

Contact Name:_____

_____

Telephone 1:_____
Telephone 2:_____

Mobile phone 1:_____
Mobile phone 2:_____

Fax:_____

E-mail 1:_____

_____

E-mail 2:_____

_____

Address 1:_____

_____

Address 2:_____

_____

How we met:_____

_____

Other details:_____

_____

_____

_____

Contact Name:_____

_____

Telephone 1:_____
Telephone 2:_____

Mobile phone 1:_____
Mobile phone 2:_____

Fax:_____

E-mail 1:_____

_____
E-mail 2:_____

_____

Address 1:_____

_____

_____
Address 2:_____

_____

How we met:_____

_____

_____
Other details:_____

_____

_____

_____

Contact Name:_____

_____

Telephone 1:_____
Telephone 2:_____

Mobile phone 1:_____
Mobile phone 2:_____

Fax:_____

E-mail 1:_____

E-mail 2:_____

_____

Address 1:_____

_____

Address 2:_____

_____

How we met:_____

_____

Other details:_____

_____

_____

_____

Contact Name: _____

_____

Telephone 1: _____
Telephone 2: _____

Mobile phone 1: _____
Mobile phone 2: _____

Fax: _____

E-mail 1: _____

_____

E-mail 2: _____

_____

Address 1: _____

_____

_____

Address 2: _____

_____

How we met: _____

_____

_____

Other details: _____

_____

_____

_____

Contact Name:_____

_____

Telephone 1:_____
Telephone 2:_____

Mobile phone 1:_____
Mobile phone 2:_____

Fax:_____

E-mail 1:_____
_____

E-mail 2:_____
_____

Address 1:_____
_____

Address 2:_____
_____

How we met:_____
_____

Other details:_____
_____
_____
_____

Contact Name:_____

_____

Telephone 1:_____
Telephone 2:_____

Mobile phone 1:_____
Mobile phone 2:_____

Fax:_____

E-mail 1:_____

_____

E-mail 2:_____

_____

Address 1:_____

_____

_____

Address 2:_____

_____

How we met:_____

_____

_____

Other details:_____

_____

_____

_____

Contact Name:_____

_____

Telephone 1:_____
Telephone 2:_____

Mobile phone 1:_____
Mobile phone 2:_____

Fax:_____

E-mail 1:_____
_____
E-mail 2:_____
_____

Address 1:_____
_____
Address 2:_____
_____

How we met:_____
_____
Other details:_____
_____
_____
_____

Contact Name: _____

_____

Telephone 1:_____
Telephone 2:_____

Mobile phone 1:_____
Mobile phone 2:_____

Fax:_____

E-mail 1:_____

_____

E-mail 2:_____

_____

Address 1:_____

_____

Address 2:_____

_____

How we met:_____

_____

_____

Other details:_____

_____

_____

_____

Contact Name: _____

_____

Telephone 1: _____
Telephone 2: _____

Mobile phone 1: _____
Mobile phone 2: _____

Fax: _____

E-mail 1: _____

E-mail 2: _____

Address 1: _____

_____

Address 2: _____

_____

How we met: _____

_____

Other details: _____

_____

_____

Contact Name: _____

_____

Telephone 1: _____
Telephone 2: _____

Mobile phone 1: _____
Mobile phone 2: _____

Fax: _____

E-mail 1: _____
_____

E-mail 2: _____
_____

Address 1: _____
_____

Address 2: _____
_____

How we met: _____
_____

Other details: _____
_____
_____
_____

Contact Name:_____

_____

Telephone 1:_____
Telephone 2:_____

Mobile phone 1:_____
Mobile phone 2:_____

Fax:_____

E-mail 1:_____

_____
E-mail 2:_____

_____

Address 1:_____

_____

Address 2:_____

_____

How we met:_____

_____

Other details:_____

_____

_____

_____

Contact Name:_____

_____

Telephone 1:_____
Telephone 2:_____

Mobile phone 1:_____
Mobile phone 2:_____

Fax:_____

E-mail 1:_____

_____

E-mail 2:_____

_____

Address 1:_____

_____

_____

Address 2:_____

_____

How we met:_____

_____

_____

Other details:_____

_____

_____

_____

Contact Name: _____

_____

Telephone 1: _____
Telephone 2: _____

Mobile phone 1: _____
Mobile phone 2: _____

Fax: _____

E-mail 1: _____

_____

E-mail 2: _____

_____

Address 1: _____

_____

Address 2: _____

_____

How we met: _____

_____

Other details: _____

_____

_____

_____

Contact Name: _____

_____

Telephone 1: _____

Telephone 2: _____

Mobile phone 1: _____

Mobile phone 2: _____

Fax: _____

E-mail 1: _____

_____

E-mail 2: _____

_____

Address 1: _____

_____

_____

Address 2: _____

_____

How we met: _____

_____

_____

Other details: _____

_____

_____

_____

Contact Name: _____

_____

Telephone 1: _____
Telephone 2: _____

Mobile phone 1: _____
Mobile phone 2: _____

Fax: _____

E-mail 1: _____

_____
E-mail 2: _____

_____

Address 1: _____

_____
Address 2: _____

_____

How we met: _____

_____
Other details: _____

_____

_____

_____

Contact Name:_____

_____

Telephone 1:_____
Telephone 2:_____

Mobile phone 1:_____
Mobile phone 2:_____

Fax:_____

E-mail 1:_____

_____

E-mail 2:_____

_____

Address 1:_____

_____

_____

Address 2:_____

_____

How we met:_____

_____

_____

Other details:_____

_____

_____

_____

Contact Name: _____

_____

Telephone 1: _____
Telephone 2: _____

Mobile phone 1: _____
Mobile phone 2: _____

Fax: _____

E-mail 1: _____
_____
E-mail 2: _____
_____

Address 1: _____
_____
Address 2: _____
_____

How we met: _____
_____
Other details: _____
_____
_____
_____

Contact Name:_____

_____

Telephone 1:_____
Telephone 2:_____

Mobile phone 1:_____
Mobile phone 2:_____

Fax:_____

E-mail 1:_____

_____

E-mail 2:_____

_____

Address 1:_____

_____

_____

Address 2:_____

_____

How we met:_____

_____

_____

Other details:_____

_____

_____

_____

Contact Name: _____

_____

Telephone 1: _____
Telephone 2: _____

Mobile phone 1: _____
Mobile phone 2: _____

Fax: _____

E-mail 1: _____

E-mail 2: _____

Address 1: _____

Address 2: _____

How we met: _____

Other details: _____

_____

_____

_____

Contact Name:_____

_____

Telephone 1:_____
Telephone 2:_____

Mobile phone 1:_____
Mobile phone 2:_____

Fax:_____

E-mail 1:_____

_____

E-mail 2:_____

_____

Address 1:_____

_____

_____

Address 2:_____

_____

How we met:_____

_____

_____

Other details:_____

_____

_____

_____

Contact Name: _____

_____

Telephone 1: _____
Telephone 2: _____

Mobile phone 1: _____
Mobile phone 2: _____

Fax: _____

E-mail 1: _____

E-mail 2: _____

_____

Address 1: _____

_____

Address 2: _____

_____

How we met: _____

_____

Other details: _____

_____

_____

_____

Contact Name:_____

_____

Telephone 1:_____
Telephone 2:_____

Mobile phone 1:_____
Mobile phone 2:_____

Fax:_____

E-mail 1:_____

_____
E-mail 2:_____

_____

Address 1:_____

_____
Address 2:_____

_____

How we met:_____

_____
Other details:_____

_____

_____

_____

Contact Name:_____

_____

Telephone 1:_____
Telephone 2:_____

Mobile phone 1:_____
Mobile phone 2:_____

Fax:_____

E-mail 1:_____

E-mail 2:_____

_____

Address 1:_____

_____

Address 2:_____

_____

How we met:_____

_____

Other details:_____

_____

_____

_____

Contact Name:_____

_____

Telephone 1:_____
Telephone 2:_____

Mobile phone 1:_____
Mobile phone 2:_____

Fax:_____

E-mail 1:_____

_____
E-mail 2:_____

_____

Address 1:_____

_____

Address 2:_____

_____

How we met:_____

_____

_____
Other details:_____

_____

_____

_____

Contact Name: _____

_____

Telephone 1: _____
Telephone 2: _____

Mobile phone 1: _____
Mobile phone 2: _____

Fax: _____

E-mail 1: _____

_____
E-mail 2: _____

_____

Address 1: _____

_____
Address 2: _____

_____

How we met: _____

_____
Other details: _____

_____

_____

_____

Contact Name: _____

_____

Telephone 1: _____

Telephone 2: _____

Mobile phone 1: _____

Mobile phone 2: _____

Fax: _____

E-mail 1: _____

_____

E-mail 2: _____

_____

Address 1: _____

_____

_____

Address 2: _____

_____

How we met: _____

_____

_____

Other details: _____

_____

_____

_____

Contact Name: _____

_____

Telephone 1: _____
Telephone 2: _____

Mobile phone 1: _____
Mobile phone 2: _____

Fax: _____

E-mail 1: _____

E-mail 2: _____

_____

Address 1: _____

_____

Address 2: _____

_____

How we met: _____

_____

Other details: _____

_____

_____

_____

Contact Name:_____

_____

Telephone 1:_____
Telephone 2:_____

Mobile phone 1:_____
Mobile phone 2:_____

Fax:_____

E-mail 1:_____

_____

E-mail 2:_____

_____

Address 1:_____

_____

Address 2:_____

_____

How we met:_____

_____

Other details:_____

_____
_____
_____

.

Contact Name:_____

_____

Telephone 1:_____
Telephone 2:_____

Mobile phone 1:_____
Mobile phone 2:_____

Fax:_____

E-mail 1:_____
_____
E-mail 2:_____
_____

Address 1:_____
_____
Address 2:_____
_____

How we met:_____
_____

Other details:_____
_____
_____
_____

Contact Name:_____

_____

Telephone 1:_____
Telephone 2:_____

Mobile phone 1:_____
Mobile phone 2:_____

Fax:_____

E-mail 1:_____

_____

E-mail 2:_____

_____

Address 1:_____

_____

_____

Address 2:_____

_____

How we met:_____

_____

_____

Other details:_____

_____

_____

_____

Contact Name: _____

_____

Telephone 1: _____
Telephone 2: _____

Mobile phone 1: _____
Mobile phone 2: _____

Fax: _____

E-mail 1: _____

_____
E-mail 2: _____

_____

Address 1: _____

_____

_____
Address 2: _____

_____

How we met: _____

_____

_____
Other details: _____

_____

_____

_____

Contact Name:_____

_____

Telephone 1:_____
Telephone 2:_____

Mobile phone 1:_____
Mobile phone 2:_____

Fax:_____

E-mail 1:_____

_____
E-mail 2:_____

_____

Address 1:_____

_____
Address 2:_____

_____

How we met:_____

_____
Other details:_____

_____

_____

_____

Contact Name: _____

_____

Telephone 1: _____

Telephone 2: _____

Mobile phone 1: _____

Mobile phone 2: _____

Fax: _____

E-mail 1: _____

_____

E-mail 2: _____

_____

Address 1: _____

_____

_____

Address 2: _____

_____

_____

How we met: _____

_____

_____

Other details: _____

_____

_____

_____

Contact Name: _____

_____

Telephone 1: _____
Telephone 2: _____

Mobile phone 1: _____
Mobile phone 2: _____

Fax: _____

E-mail 1: _____

_____

E-mail 2: _____

_____

Address 1: _____

_____

_____

Address 2: _____

_____

How we met: _____

_____

_____

Other details: _____

_____

_____

_____

Contact Name: _____

_____

Telephone 1: _____
Telephone 2: _____

Mobile phone 1: _____
Mobile phone 2: _____

Fax: _____

E-mail 1: _____

E-mail 2: _____

_____

Address 1: _____

_____

Address 2: _____

_____

How we met: _____

_____

Other details: _____

_____

_____

_____

Contact Name:_____

_____

Telephone 1:_____
Telephone 2:_____

Mobile phone 1:_____
Mobile phone 2:_____

Fax:_____

E-mail 1:_____

_____

E-mail 2:_____

_____

Address 1:_____

_____

Address 2:_____

_____

How we met:_____

_____

_____

Other details:_____

_____

_____

_____

Contact Name: _____

_____

Telephone 1: _____

Telephone 2: _____

Mobile phone 1: _____

Mobile phone 2: _____

Fax: _____

E-mail 1: _____

_____

E-mail 2: _____

_____

Address 1: _____

_____

Address 2: _____

_____

How we met: _____

_____

Other details: _____

_____

_____

_____

Contact Name:_____

_____

Telephone 1:_____
Telephone 2:_____

Mobile phone 1:_____
Mobile phone 2:_____

Fax:_____

E-mail 1:_____

_____

E-mail 2:_____

_____

Address 1:_____

_____

_____

Address 2:_____

_____

How we met:_____

_____

_____

Other details:_____

_____

_____

_____

Contact Name: _____

_____

Telephone 1: _____
Telephone 2: _____

Mobile phone 1: _____
Mobile phone 2: _____

Fax: _____

E-mail 1: _____

_____

E-mail 2: _____

_____

Address 1: _____

_____

_____

Address 2: _____

_____

How we met: _____

_____

_____

Other details: _____

_____

_____

_____

Contact Name:_____

_____

Telephone 1:_____
Telephone 2:_____

Mobile phone 1:_____
Mobile phone 2:_____

Fax:_____

E-mail 1:_____

_____

E-mail 2:_____

_____

Address 1:_____

_____

_____

Address 2:_____

_____

How we met:_____

_____

_____

Other details:_____

_____

_____

_____

Contact Name:_____

_____

Telephone 1:_____
Telephone 2:_____

Mobile phone 1:_____
Mobile phone 2:_____

Fax:_____

E-mail 1:_____
_____
E-mail 2:_____
_____

Address 1:_____
_____
Address 2:_____
_____

How we met:_____
_____
Other details:_____
_____
_____
_____

Contact Name:_____

_____

Telephone 1:_____
Telephone 2:_____

Mobile phone 1:_____
Mobile phone 2:_____

Fax:_____

E-mail 1:_____

_____

E-mail 2:_____

_____

Address 1:_____

_____

Address 2:_____

_____

How we met:_____

_____

Other details:_____

_____

_____

_____

Contact Name: _____

_____

Telephone 1: _____
Telephone 2: _____

Mobile phone 1: _____
Mobile phone 2: _____

Fax: _____

E-mail 1: _____

_____
E-mail 2: _____

_____

Address 1: _____

_____

_____
Address 2: _____

_____

How we met: _____

_____

_____
Other details: _____

_____

_____

_____

Contact Name: _____

_____

Telephone 1: _____
Telephone 2: _____

Mobile phone 1: _____
Mobile phone 2: _____

Fax: _____

E-mail 1: _____

_____
E-mail 2: _____

_____

Address 1: _____

_____

_____
Address 2: _____

_____

How we met: _____

_____

_____
Other details: _____

_____

_____

_____

Contact Name: _____

_____

Telephone 1: _____
Telephone 2: _____

Mobile phone 1: _____
Mobile phone 2: _____

Fax: _____

E-mail 1: _____

E-mail 2: _____

_____

Address 1: _____

_____

Address 2: _____

_____

How we met: _____

_____

Other details: _____

_____

_____

_____

Contact Name:_____

_____

Telephone 1:_____
Telephone 2:_____

Mobile phone 1:_____
Mobile phone 2:_____

Fax:_____

E-mail 1:_____

_____

E-mail 2:_____

_____

Address 1:_____

_____

_____

Address 2:_____

_____

How we met:_____

_____

_____

Other details:_____

_____

_____

_____

Contact Name:_____

_____

Telephone 1:_____
Telephone 2:_____

Mobile phone 1:_____
Mobile phone 2:_____

Fax:_____

E-mail 1:_____

_____
E-mail 2:_____

_____

Address 1:_____

_____

_____
Address 2:_____

_____

How we met:_____

_____

_____
Other details:_____

_____

_____

_____

Contact Name: _____

_____

Telephone 1: _____
Telephone 2: _____

Mobile phone 1: _____
Mobile phone 2: _____

Fax: _____

E-mail 1: _____

_____

E-mail 2: _____

_____

Address 1: _____

_____

_____

Address 2: _____

_____

How we met: _____

_____

_____

Other details: _____

_____

_____

_____

Contact Name:_____

_____

Telephone 1:_____
Telephone 2:_____

Mobile phone 1:_____
Mobile phone 2:_____

Fax:_____

E-mail 1:_____

_____
E-mail 2:_____

_____

Address 1:_____

_____

Address 2:_____

_____

How we met:_____

_____

Other details:_____

_____

_____

_____

Contact Name:_____

_____

Telephone 1:_____
Telephone 2:_____

Mobile phone 1:_____
Mobile phone 2:_____

Fax:_____

E-mail 1:_____

_____
E-mail 2:_____

_____

Address 1:_____

_____

_____
Address 2:_____

_____

How we met:_____

_____

_____
Other details:_____

_____

_____

_____

Contact Name:_____

_____

Telephone 1:_____
Telephone 2:_____

Mobile phone 1:_____
Mobile phone 2:_____

Fax:_____

E-mail 1:_____

E-mail 2:_____

Address 1:_____

Address 2:_____

How we met:_____

Other details:_____

_____

_____

Contact Name: _____

_____

Telephone 1: _____

Telephone 2: _____

Mobile phone 1: _____

Mobile phone 2: _____

Fax: _____

E-mail 1: _____

_____

E-mail 2: _____

_____

Address 1: _____

_____

_____

Address 2: _____

_____

How we met: _____

_____

_____

Other details: _____

_____

_____

_____

Contact Name: _____

_____

Telephone 1: _____
Telephone 2: _____

Mobile phone 1: _____
Mobile phone 2: _____

Fax: _____

E-mail 1: _____

_____

E-mail 2: _____

_____

Address 1: _____

_____

Address 2: _____

_____

How we met: _____

_____

Other details: _____

_____

_____

_____

Contact Name: _____

_____

Telephone 1: _____
Telephone 2: _____

Mobile phone 1: _____
Mobile phone 2: _____

Fax: _____

E-mail 1: _____

_____

E-mail 2: _____

_____

Address 1: _____

_____

_____

Address 2: _____

_____

How we met: _____

_____

_____

Other details: _____

_____

_____

_____

Contact Name: _____

_____

Telephone 1: _____
Telephone 2: _____

Mobile phone 1: _____
Mobile phone 2: _____

Fax: _____

E-mail 1: _____

_____
E-mail 2: _____

_____

Address 1: _____

_____
Address 2: _____

_____

How we met: _____

_____
Other details: _____

_____

_____

_____

Contact Name: _____

_____

Telephone 1: _____
Telephone 2: _____

Mobile phone 1: _____
Mobile phone 2: _____

Fax: _____

E-mail 1: _____

_____
E-mail 2: _____

_____

Address 1: _____

_____

_____
Address 2: _____

_____

How we met: _____

_____

_____
Other details: _____

_____

_____

_____

Contact Name:_____

_____

Telephone 1:_____
Telephone 2:_____

Mobile phone 1:_____
Mobile phone 2:_____

Fax:_____

E-mail 1:_____

_____

E-mail 2:_____

_____

Address 1:_____

_____

_____

Address 2:_____

_____

How we met:_____

_____

_____

Other details:_____

_____

_____

_____

Contact Name: _____

_____

Telephone 1: _____
Telephone 2: _____

Mobile phone 1: _____
Mobile phone 2: _____

Fax: _____

E-mail 1: _____

_____

E-mail 2: _____

_____

Address 1: _____

_____

_____

Address 2: _____

_____

How we met: _____

_____

_____

Other details: _____

_____

_____

_____

Contact Name: _____

_____

Telephone 1: _____
Telephone 2: _____

Mobile phone 1: _____
Mobile phone 2: _____

Fax: _____

E-mail 1: _____

E-mail 2: _____

_____

Address 1: _____

_____

Address 2: _____

_____

How we met: _____

_____

Other details: _____

_____

_____

_____

Contact Name:_____

_____

Telephone 1:_____
Telephone 2:_____

Mobile phone 1:_____
Mobile phone 2:_____

Fax:_____

E-mail 1:_____

_____

E-mail 2:_____

_____

Address 1:_____

_____

_____

Address 2:_____

_____

How we met:_____

_____

_____

Other details:_____

_____

_____

_____

Contact Name:_____

_____

Telephone 1:_____
Telephone 2:_____

Mobile phone 1:_____
Mobile phone 2:_____

Fax:_____

E-mail 1:_____

_____
E-mail 2:_____

_____

Address 1:_____

_____

Address 2:_____

_____

How we met:_____

_____

Other details:_____

_____

_____

_____

Contact Name: _____

_____

Telephone 1:_____
Telephone 2:_____

Mobile phone 1:_____
Mobile phone 2:_____

Fax:_____

E-mail 1:_____

_____

E-mail 2:_____

_____

Address 1:_____

_____

_____

Address 2:_____

_____

How we met:_____

_____

_____

Other details:_____

_____

_____

_____

Contact Name:_____

_____

Telephone 1:_____
Telephone 2:_____

Mobile phone 1:_____
Mobile phone 2:_____

Fax:_____

E-mail 1:_____
_____
E-mail 2:_____
_____

Address 1:_____
_____
_____
Address 2:_____
_____

How we met:_____
_____
_____
Other details:_____
_____
_____
_____

Contact Name: _____

_____

Telephone 1: _____
Telephone 2: _____

Mobile phone 1: _____
Mobile phone 2: _____

Fax: _____

E-mail 1: _____

_____

E-mail 2: _____

_____

Address 1: _____

_____

Address 2: _____

_____

How we met: _____

_____

Other details: _____

_____

_____

_____

Contact Name:_____

_____

Telephone 1:_____
Telephone 2:_____

Mobile phone 1:_____
Mobile phone 2:_____

Fax:_____

E-mail 1:_____

_____

E-mail 2:_____

_____

Address 1:_____

_____

Address 2:_____

_____

How we met:_____

_____

Other details:_____

_____

_____

_____

Contact Name:_____

_____

Telephone 1:_____
Telephone 2:_____

Mobile phone 1:_____
Mobile phone 2:_____

Fax:_____

E-mail 1:_____

_____

E-mail 2:_____

_____

Address 1:_____

_____

Address 2:_____

_____

How we met:_____

_____

Other details:_____

_____

_____

_____

Contact Name:_____

_____

Telephone 1:_____
Telephone 2:_____

Mobile phone 1:_____
Mobile phone 2:_____

Fax:_____

E-mail 1:_____

E-mail 2:_____

_____

Address 1:_____

_____

Address 2:_____

_____

How we met:_____

_____

Other details:_____

_____

_____

_____

Contact Name: _____

_____

Telephone 1: _____
Telephone 2: _____

Mobile phone 1: _____
Mobile phone 2: _____

Fax: _____

E-mail 1: _____

_____

E-mail 2: _____

_____

Address 1: _____

_____

Address 2: _____

_____

How we met: _____

_____

Other details: _____

_____

_____

_____

Contact Name:_____

_____

Telephone 1:_____
Telephone 2:_____

Mobile phone 1:_____
Mobile phone 2:_____

Fax:_____

E-mail 1:_____
_____
E-mail 2:_____

_____

Address 1:_____
_____
_____
Address 2:_____

_____

How we met:_____
_____
_____
Other details:_____

_____

_____

_____

Contact Name:_____

_____

Telephone 1:_____
Telephone 2:_____

Mobile phone 1:_____
Mobile phone 2:_____

Fax:_____

E-mail 1:_____

_____

E-mail 2:_____

_____

Address 1:_____

_____

_____

Address 2:_____

_____

How we met:_____

_____

_____

Other details:_____

_____

_____

_____

Contact Name:_____

_____

Telephone 1:_____
Telephone 2:_____

Mobile phone 1:_____
Mobile phone 2:_____

Fax:_____

E-mail 1:_____

_____
E-mail 2:_____

_____

Address 1:_____

_____

Address 2:_____

_____

How we met:_____

_____

Other details:_____

_____

_____

_____

Contact Name: _____

_____

Telephone 1: _____
Telephone 2: _____

Mobile phone 1: _____
Mobile phone 2: _____

Fax: _____

E-mail 1: _____

_____

E-mail 2: _____

_____

Address 1: _____

_____

_____

Address 2: _____

_____

How we met: _____

_____

_____

Other details: _____

_____

_____

_____

Contact Name: _____

_____

Telephone 1: _____
Telephone 2: _____

Mobile phone 1: _____
Mobile phone 2: _____

Fax: _____

E-mail 1: _____

E-mail 2: _____

Address 1: _____

Address 2: _____

How we met: _____

Other details: _____

Contact Name: _____

_____

Telephone 1: _____
Telephone 2: _____

Mobile phone 1: _____
Mobile phone 2: _____

Fax: _____

E-mail 1: _____

_____
E-mail 2: _____

_____

Address 1: _____

_____

_____
Address 2: _____

_____

How we met: _____

_____

_____
Other details: _____

_____

_____

_____

Contact Name: _____

_____

Telephone 1: _____
Telephone 2: _____

Mobile phone 1: _____
Mobile phone 2: _____

Fax: _____

E-mail 1: _____

E-mail 2: _____

_____

Address 1: _____

_____

Address 2: _____

_____

How we met: _____

_____

Other details: _____

_____

_____

_____

Contact Name:_____

_____

Telephone 1:_____
Telephone 2:_____

Mobile phone 1:_____
Mobile phone 2:_____

Fax:_____

E-mail 1:_____

_____
E-mail 2:_____

_____

Address 1:_____

_____

_____
Address 2:_____

_____

How we met:_____

_____

_____
Other details:_____

_____

_____

_____

Contact Name:_____

_____

Telephone 1:_____
Telephone 2:_____

Mobile phone 1:_____
Mobile phone 2:_____

Fax:_____

E-mail 1:_____
_____
E-mail 2:_____
_____

Address 1:_____
_____
Address 2:_____
_____

How we met:_____
_____

Other details:_____
_____
_____
_____

Contact Name:_____

_____

Telephone 1:_____
Telephone 2:_____

Mobile phone 1:_____
Mobile phone 2:_____

Fax:_____

E-mail 1:_____

_____

E-mail 2:_____

_____

Address 1:_____

_____

_____

Address 2:_____

_____

How we met:_____

_____

_____

Other details:_____

_____

_____

_____

Contact Name:_____

_____

Telephone 1:_____
Telephone 2:_____

Mobile phone 1:_____
Mobile phone 2:_____

Fax:_____

E-mail 1:_____

_____
E-mail 2:_____

_____

Address 1:_____

_____

Address 2:_____

_____

How we met:_____

_____

Other details:_____

_____

_____

_____

Contact Name: _____

_____

Telephone 1: _____
Telephone 2: _____

Mobile phone 1: _____
Mobile phone 2: _____

Fax: _____

E-mail 1: _____

_____

E-mail 2: _____

_____

Address 1: _____

_____

Address 2: _____

_____

How we met: _____

_____

Other details: _____

_____

_____

_____

Contact Name:_____

_____

Telephone 1:_____
Telephone 2:_____

Mobile phone 1:_____
Mobile phone 2:_____

Fax:_____

E-mail 1:_____
_____

E-mail 2:_____
_____

Address 1:_____
_____
_____

Address 2:_____
_____

How we met:_____
_____
_____

Other details:_____
_____
_____
_____

Contact Name:_____

_____

Telephone 1:_____
Telephone 2:_____

Mobile phone 1:_____
Mobile phone 2:_____

Fax:_____

E-mail 1:_____

_____

E-mail 2:_____

_____

Address 1:_____

_____

_____

Address 2:_____

_____

How we met:_____

_____

_____

Other details:_____

_____

_____

_____

Contact Name:_____

_____

Telephone 1:_____
Telephone 2:_____

Mobile phone 1:_____
Mobile phone 2:_____

Fax:_____

E-mail 1:_____

E-mail 2:_____

_____

Address 1:_____

_____

Address 2:_____

_____

How we met:_____

_____

Other details:_____

_____

_____

_____

Contact Name:_____

_____

Telephone 1:_____
Telephone 2:_____

Mobile phone 1:_____
Mobile phone 2:_____

Fax:_____

E-mail 1:_____

_____

E-mail 2:_____

_____

Address 1:_____

_____

Address 2:_____

_____

How we met:_____

_____

Other details:_____

_____

_____

_____

Contact Name:_____

_____

Telephone 1:_____
Telephone 2:_____

Mobile phone 1:_____
Mobile phone 2:_____

Fax:_____

E-mail 1:_____

_____

E-mail 2:_____

_____

Address 1:_____

_____

_____

Address 2:_____

_____

How we met:_____

_____

_____

Other details:_____

_____

_____

_____

Contact Name: _____

_____

Telephone 1: _____
Telephone 2: _____

Mobile phone 1: _____
Mobile phone 2: _____

Fax: _____

E-mail 1: _____

_____
E-mail 2: _____

_____

Address 1: _____

_____

_____
Address 2: _____

_____

How we met: _____

_____

_____
Other details: _____

_____

_____

_____

Contact Name:_____

_____

Telephone 1:_____
Telephone 2:_____

Mobile phone 1:_____
Mobile phone 2:_____

Fax:_____

E-mail 1:_____

E-mail 2:_____

_____

Address 1:_____

_____

Address 2:_____

_____

How we met:_____

_____

Other details:_____

_____

_____

_____

Contact Name: _____

_____

Telephone 1: _____
Telephone 2: _____

Mobile phone 1: _____
Mobile phone 2: _____

Fax: _____

E-mail 1: _____

_____

E-mail 2: _____

_____

Address 1: _____

_____

Address 2: _____

_____

How we met: _____

_____

Other details: _____

_____

_____

_____

Contact Name: _____

_____

Telephone 1: _____
Telephone 2: _____

Mobile phone 1: _____
Mobile phone 2: _____

Fax: _____

E-mail 1: _____
_____

E-mail 2: _____
_____

Address 1: _____
_____

Address 2: _____
_____

How we met: _____
_____

Other details: _____
_____
_____
_____

Contact Name: _____

_____

Telephone 1: _____
Telephone 2: _____

Mobile phone 1: _____
Mobile phone 2: _____

Fax: _____

E-mail 1: _____

_____

E-mail 2: _____

_____

Address 1: _____

_____

Address 2: _____

_____

How we met: _____

_____

Other details: _____

_____

_____

_____

Contact Name:_____

_____

Telephone 1:_____
Telephone 2:_____

Mobile phone 1:_____
Mobile phone 2:_____

Fax:_____

E-mail 1:_____

E-mail 2:_____

Address 1:_____

_____

Address 2:_____

_____

How we met:_____

_____

Other details:_____

_____

_____

_____

Contact Name: _____

_____

Telephone 1: _____
Telephone 2: _____

Mobile phone 1: _____
Mobile phone 2: _____

Fax: _____

E-mail 1: _____

_____

E-mail 2: _____

_____

Address 1: _____

_____

Address 2: _____

_____

How we met: _____

_____

Other details: _____

_____

_____

_____

Contact Name:_____

_____

Telephone 1:_____
Telephone 2:_____

Mobile phone 1:_____
Mobile phone 2:_____

Fax:_____

E-mail 1:_____
_____

E-mail 2:_____
_____

Address 1:_____
_____

Address 2:_____
_____

How we met:_____
_____

Other details:_____
_____
_____
_____

Contact Name:_____

_____

Telephone 1:_____
Telephone 2:_____

Mobile phone 1:_____
Mobile phone 2:_____

Fax:_____

E-mail 1:_____

_____

E-mail 2:_____

_____

Address 1:_____

_____

Address 2:_____

_____

How we met:_____

_____

Other details:_____

_____

_____

_____

Contact Name: _____

_____

Telephone 1: _____
Telephone 2: _____

Mobile phone 1: _____
Mobile phone 2: _____

Fax: _____

E-mail 1: _____

E-mail 2: _____

_____

Address 1: _____

_____

Address 2: _____

_____

How we met: _____

_____

Other details: _____

_____

_____

_____

Contact Name:_____

_____

Telephone 1:_____
Telephone 2:_____

Mobile phone 1:_____
Mobile phone 2:_____

Fax:_____

E-mail 1:_____

_____

E-mail 2:_____

_____

Address 1:_____

_____

_____

Address 2:_____

_____

How we met:_____

_____

_____

Other details:_____

_____

_____

_____

Contact Name:_____

_____

Telephone 1:_____
Telephone 2:_____

Mobile phone 1:_____
Mobile phone 2:_____

Fax:_____

E-mail 1:_____

_____
E-mail 2:_____

_____

Address 1:_____

_____

_____
Address 2:_____

_____

How we met:_____

_____

_____
Other details:_____

_____

_____

_____

Contact Name: _____

_____

Telephone 1: _____
Telephone 2: _____

Mobile phone 1: _____
Mobile phone 2: _____

Fax: _____

E-mail 1: _____

_____

E-mail 2: _____

_____

Address 1: _____

_____

Address 2: _____

_____

How we met: _____

_____

Other details: _____

_____

_____

_____

Contact Name:_____

_____

Telephone 1:_____
Telephone 2:_____

Mobile phone 1:_____
Mobile phone 2:_____

Fax:_____

E-mail 1:_____

E-mail 2:_____

_____

Address 1:_____

_____

Address 2:_____

_____

How we met:_____

_____

Other details:_____

_____

_____

_____

Contact Name: _____

_____

Telephone 1: _____
Telephone 2: _____

Mobile phone 1: _____
Mobile phone 2: _____

Fax: _____

E-mail 1: _____

_____

E-mail 2: _____

_____

Address 1: _____

_____

_____

Address 2: _____

_____

How we met: _____

_____

_____

Other details: _____

_____

_____

_____

Contact Name:_____

_____

Telephone 1:_____
Telephone 2:_____

Mobile phone 1:_____
Mobile phone 2:_____

Fax:_____

E-mail 1:_____

_____

E-mail 2:_____

_____

Address 1:_____

_____

Address 2:_____

_____

How we met:_____

_____

Other details:_____

_____

_____

_____

Contact Name:_____

_____

Telephone 1:_____
Telephone 2:_____

Mobile phone 1:_____
Mobile phone 2:_____

Fax:_____

E-mail 1:_____

_____

E-mail 2:_____

_____

Address 1:_____

_____

_____

Address 2:_____

_____

How we met:_____

_____

_____

Other details:_____

_____

_____

_____

Contact Name:_____

_____

Telephone 1:_____
Telephone 2:_____

Mobile phone 1:_____
Mobile phone 2:_____

Fax:_____

E-mail 1:_____

E-mail 2:_____

_____

Address 1:_____

_____

Address 2:_____

_____

How we met:_____

_____

Other details:_____

_____

_____

_____

Contact Name:_____

_____

Telephone 1:_____
Telephone 2:_____

Mobile phone 1:_____
Mobile phone 2:_____

Fax:_____

E-mail 1:_____

_____

E-mail 2:_____

_____

Address 1:_____

_____

Address 2:_____

_____

How we met:_____

_____

Other details:_____

_____

_____

_____

Contact Name: _____

_____

Telephone 1: _____
Telephone 2: _____

Mobile phone 1: _____
Mobile phone 2: _____

Fax: _____

E-mail 1: _____

_____
E-mail 2: _____

_____

Address 1: _____

_____
_____
Address 2: _____

_____

How we met: _____

_____
_____
Other details: _____

_____
_____
_____

Contact Name: _____

_____

Telephone 1: _____
Telephone 2: _____

Mobile phone 1: _____
Mobile phone 2: _____

Fax: _____

E-mail 1: _____

_____

E-mail 2: _____

_____

Address 1: _____

_____

_____

Address 2: _____

_____

How we met: _____

_____

_____

Other details: _____

_____

_____

_____

Contact Name:_____

_____

Telephone 1:_____
Telephone 2:_____

Mobile phone 1:_____
Mobile phone 2:_____

Fax:_____

E-mail 1:_____

_____
E-mail 2:_____

_____

Address 1:_____

_____

Address 2:_____

_____

How we met:_____

_____

Other details:_____

_____

_____

_____

Contact Name:_____

_____

Telephone 1:_____
Telephone 2:_____

Mobile phone 1:_____
Mobile phone 2:_____

Fax:_____

E-mail 1:_____

_____
E-mail 2:_____

_____

Address 1:_____

_____
_____
Address 2:_____

_____

How we met:_____

_____
_____
Other details:_____

_____
_____
_____

Contact Name:_____

_____

Telephone 1:_____
Telephone 2:_____

Mobile phone 1:_____
Mobile phone 2:_____

Fax:_____

E-mail 1:_____

_____

E-mail 2:_____

_____

Address 1:_____

_____

Address 2:_____

_____

How we met:_____

_____

Other details:_____

_____

_____

_____

Contact Name:_____

_____

Telephone 1:_____
Telephone 2:_____

Mobile phone 1:_____
Mobile phone 2:_____

Fax:_____

E-mail 1:_____

_____

E-mail 2:_____

_____

Address 1:_____

_____

_____

Address 2:_____

_____

How we met:_____

_____

_____

Other details:_____

_____

_____

_____

Contact Name: _____

_____

Telephone 1: _____
Telephone 2: _____

Mobile phone 1: _____
Mobile phone 2: _____

Fax: _____

E-mail 1: _____
_____
E-mail 2: _____
_____

Address 1: _____
_____
_____
Address 2: _____
_____

How we met: _____
_____
_____
Other details: _____
_____
_____
_____

Contact Name:_____

_____

Telephone 1:_____

Telephone 2:_____

Mobile phone 1:_____

Mobile phone 2:_____

Fax:_____

E-mail 1:_____

_____

E-mail 2:_____

_____

Address 1:_____

_____

Address 2:_____

_____

How we met:_____

_____

Other details:_____

_____

_____

_____

Contact Name:_____

_____

Telephone 1:_____
Telephone 2:_____

Mobile phone 1:_____
Mobile phone 2:_____

Fax:_____

E-mail 1:_____

_____
E-mail 2:_____

_____

Address 1:_____

_____
Address 2:_____

_____

How we met:_____

_____
Other details:_____

_____
_____
_____

Contact Name: _____

_____

Telephone 1: _____
Telephone 2: _____

Mobile phone 1: _____
Mobile phone 2: _____

Fax: _____

E-mail 1: _____

_____

E-mail 2: _____

_____

Address 1: _____

_____

_____

Address 2: _____

_____

How we met: _____

_____

_____

Other details: _____

_____

_____

_____

Contact Name:_____

_____

Telephone 1:_____
Telephone 2:_____

Mobile phone 1:_____
Mobile phone 2:_____

Fax:_____

E-mail 1:_____

_____

E-mail 2:_____

_____

Address 1:_____

_____

_____

Address 2:_____

_____

How we met:_____

_____

_____

Other details:_____

_____

_____

_____

Contact Name:_____

_____

Telephone 1:_____
Telephone 2:_____

Mobile phone 1:_____
Mobile phone 2:_____

Fax:_____

E-mail 1:_____

_____
E-mail 2:_____

_____

Address 1:_____

_____

_____
Address 2:_____

_____

How we met:_____

_____

_____
Other details:_____

_____

_____

_____

Contact Name: _____

_____

Telephone 1: _____
Telephone 2: _____

Mobile phone 1: _____
Mobile phone 2: _____

Fax: _____

E-mail 1: _____
_____

E-mail 2: _____
_____

Address 1: _____
_____
_____

Address 2: _____
_____

How we met: _____
_____
_____

Other details: _____
_____
_____
_____

Contact Name: _____

_____

Telephone 1: _____
Telephone 2: _____

Mobile phone 1: _____
Mobile phone 2: _____

Fax: _____

E-mail 1: _____

_____

E-mail 2: _____

_____

Address 1: _____

_____

_____

Address 2: _____

_____

How we met: _____

_____

_____

Other details: _____

_____

_____

_____

Contact Name:_____

_____

Telephone 1:_____
Telephone 2:_____

Mobile phone 1:_____
Mobile phone 2:_____

Fax:_____

E-mail 1:_____

_____
E-mail 2:_____

_____

Address 1:_____

_____
Address 2:_____

_____

How we met:_____

_____
Other details:_____

_____

_____

_____

Contact Name:_____

_____

Telephone 1:_____
Telephone 2:_____

Mobile phone 1:_____
Mobile phone 2:_____

Fax:_____

E-mail 1:_____

_____
E-mail 2:_____

_____

Address 1:_____

_____

_____
Address 2:_____

_____

How we met:_____

_____

_____
Other details:_____

_____

_____

_____

Contact Name: _____

_____

Telephone 1: _____
Telephone 2: _____

Mobile phone 1: _____
Mobile phone 2: _____

Fax: _____

E-mail 1: _____

_____
E-mail 2: _____

_____

Address 1: _____

_____
Address 2: _____

_____

How we met: _____

_____
Other details: _____

_____

_____

_____

Contact Name:_____

_____

Telephone 1:_____
Telephone 2:_____

Mobile phone 1:_____
Mobile phone 2:_____

Fax:_____

E-mail 1:_____

_____

E-mail 2:_____

_____

Address 1:_____

_____

_____

Address 2:_____

_____

How we met:_____

_____

_____

Other details:_____

_____

_____

_____

Contact Name: _____

_____

Telephone 1: _____
Telephone 2: _____

Mobile phone 1: _____
Mobile phone 2: _____

Fax: _____

E-mail 1: _____

E-mail 2: _____
_____

Address 1: _____
_____

Address 2: _____
_____

How we met: _____
_____

Other details: _____
_____
_____
_____

Contact Name: _____

_____

Telephone 1: _____
Telephone 2: _____

Mobile phone 1: _____
Mobile phone 2: _____

Fax: _____

E-mail 1: _____

_____

E-mail 2: _____

_____

Address 1: _____

_____

_____

Address 2: _____

_____

How we met: _____

_____

_____

Other details: _____

_____

_____

_____

Contact Name: _____

_____

Telephone 1: _____

Telephone 2: _____

Mobile phone 1: _____

Mobile phone 2: _____

Fax: _____

E-mail 1: _____

E-mail 2: _____

_____

Address 1: _____

_____

Address 2: _____

_____

How we met: _____

_____

Other details: _____

_____

_____

_____

Contact Name: _____

_____

Telephone 1: _____
Telephone 2: _____

Mobile phone 1: _____
Mobile phone 2: _____

Fax: _____

E-mail 1: _____

_____

E-mail 2: _____

_____

Address 1: _____

_____

_____

Address 2: _____

_____

How we met: _____

_____

_____

Other details: _____

_____

_____

_____

Contact Name: _____

_____

Telephone 1: _____
Telephone 2: _____

Mobile phone 1: _____
Mobile phone 2: _____

Fax: _____

E-mail 1: _____

_____

E-mail 2: _____

_____

Address 1: _____

_____

Address 2: _____

_____

How we met: _____

_____

Other details: _____

_____

_____

_____

Contact Name:_____

_____

Telephone 1:_____
Telephone 2:_____

Mobile phone 1:_____
Mobile phone 2:_____

Fax:_____

E-mail 1:_____

_____

E-mail 2:_____

_____

Address 1:_____

_____

Address 2:_____

_____

How we met:_____

_____

Other details:_____

_____

_____

_____

Contact Name: _____

_____

Telephone 1: _____
Telephone 2: _____

Mobile phone 1: _____
Mobile phone 2: _____

Fax: _____

E-mail 1: _____

_____

E-mail 2: _____

_____

Address 1: _____

_____

_____

Address 2: _____

_____

How we met: _____

_____

_____

Other details: _____

_____

_____

_____

Contact Name:_____

_____

Telephone 1:_____
Telephone 2:_____

Mobile phone 1:_____
Mobile phone 2:_____

Fax:_____

E-mail 1:_____

_____
E-mail 2:_____

_____

Address 1:_____

_____

_____
Address 2:_____

_____

How we met:_____

_____

_____
Other details:_____

_____

_____

_____

Contact Name:_____

_____

Telephone 1:_____
Telephone 2:_____

Mobile phone 1:_____
Mobile phone 2:_____

Fax:_____

E-mail 1:_____

E-mail 2:_____

_____

Address 1:_____

_____

Address 2:_____

_____

How we met:_____

_____

Other details:_____

_____

_____

_____

Contact Name:_____

_____

Telephone 1:_____
Telephone 2:_____

Mobile phone 1:_____
Mobile phone 2:_____

Fax:_____

E-mail 1:_____

_____

E-mail 2:_____

_____

Address 1:_____

_____

_____

Address 2:_____

_____

How we met:_____

_____

_____

Other details:_____

_____

_____

_____

Contact Name:_____

_____

Telephone 1:_____
Telephone 2:_____

Mobile phone 1:_____
Mobile phone 2:_____

Fax:_____

E-mail 1:_____

_____
E-mail 2:_____

_____

Address 1:_____

_____

_____
Address 2:_____

_____

How we met:_____

_____

_____
Other details:_____

_____

_____

_____

Contact Name:_____

_____

Telephone 1:_____
Telephone 2:_____

Mobile phone 1:_____
Mobile phone 2:_____

Fax:_____

E-mail 1:_____

_____

E-mail 2:_____

_____

Address 1:_____

_____

Address 2:_____

_____

How we met:_____

_____

Other details:_____

_____

_____

_____

Contact Name: _____

_____

Telephone 1: _____
Telephone 2: _____

Mobile phone 1: _____
Mobile phone 2: _____

Fax: _____

E-mail 1: _____

_____
E-mail 2: _____

_____

Address 1: _____

_____

_____
Address 2: _____

_____

How we met: _____

_____

_____
Other details: _____

_____

_____

_____

Contact Name:_____

_____

Telephone 1:_____
Telephone 2:_____

Mobile phone 1:_____
Mobile phone 2:_____

Fax:_____

E-mail 1:_____

_____
E-mail 2:_____

_____

Address 1:_____

_____

_____
Address 2:_____

_____

How we met:_____

_____

_____
Other details:_____

_____

_____

_____

Contact Name: _____

_____

Telephone 1: _____
Telephone 2: _____

Mobile phone 1: _____
Mobile phone 2: _____

Fax: _____

E-mail 1: _____
_____
E-mail 2: _____
_____

Address 1: _____
_____
Address 2: _____
_____

How we met: _____
_____
Other details: _____
_____
_____
_____

Contact Name: _____

_____

Telephone 1: _____
Telephone 2: _____

Mobile phone 1: _____
Mobile phone 2: _____

Fax: _____

E-mail 1: _____

_____

E-mail 2: _____

_____

Address 1: _____

_____

_____

Address 2: _____

_____

How we met: _____

_____

_____

Other details: _____

_____

_____

_____

Contact Name: _____

_____

Telephone 1: _____
Telephone 2: _____

Mobile phone 1: _____
Mobile phone 2: _____

Fax: _____

E-mail 1: _____

_____

E-mail 2: _____

_____

Address 1: _____

_____

Address 2: _____

_____

How we met: _____

_____

Other details: _____

_____

_____

_____

Contact Name: _____

_____

Telephone 1: _____
Telephone 2: _____

Mobile phone 1: _____
Mobile phone 2: _____

Fax: _____

E-mail 1: _____

_____
E-mail 2: _____

_____

Address 1: _____

_____

_____
Address 2: _____

_____

How we met: _____

_____

_____
Other details: _____

_____

_____

_____

Contact Name: _____

_____

Telephone 1: _____
Telephone 2: _____

Mobile phone 1: _____
Mobile phone 2: _____

Fax: _____

E-mail 1: _____
_____

E-mail 2: _____
_____

Address 1: _____
_____
_____

Address 2: _____
_____

How we met: _____
_____
_____

Other details: _____
_____
_____
_____

Contact Name:_____

_____

Telephone 1:_____
Telephone 2:_____

Mobile phone 1:_____
Mobile phone 2:_____

Fax:_____

E-mail 1:_____

_____
E-mail 2:_____

_____

Address 1:_____

_____

Address 2:_____

_____

How we met:_____

_____

Other details:_____

_____

_____

_____

Contact Name:_____

_____

Telephone 1:_____
Telephone 2:_____

Mobile phone 1:_____
Mobile phone 2:_____

Fax:_____

E-mail 1:_____

_____

E-mail 2:_____

_____

Address 1:_____

_____

Address 2:_____

_____

How we met:_____

_____

Other details:_____

_____

_____

_____

Contact Name:_____

_____

Telephone 1:_____
Telephone 2:_____

Mobile phone 1:_____
Mobile phone 2:_____

Fax:_____

E-mail 1:_____

_____

E-mail 2:_____

_____

Address 1:_____

_____

_____

Address 2:_____

_____

How we met:_____

_____

_____

Other details:_____

_____

_____

_____

Contact Name:_____

_____

Telephone 1:_____
Telephone 2:_____

Mobile phone 1:_____
Mobile phone 2:_____

Fax:_____

E-mail 1:_____

E-mail 2:_____

_____

Address 1:_____

_____

Address 2:_____

_____

How we met:_____

_____

Other details:_____

_____

_____

_____

Contact Name:_____

_____

Telephone 1:_____
Telephone 2:_____

Mobile phone 1:_____
Mobile phone 2:_____

Fax:_____

E-mail 1:_____

_____
E-mail 2:_____

_____

Address 1:_____

_____

_____
Address 2:_____

_____

How we met:_____

_____

_____
Other details:_____

_____

_____

_____

Contact Name: _____

_____

Telephone 1: _____
Telephone 2: _____

Mobile phone 1: _____
Mobile phone 2: _____

Fax: _____

E-mail 1: _____
_____

E-mail 2: _____
_____

Address 1: _____
_____

Address 2: _____
_____

How we met: _____
_____

Other details: _____
_____
_____
_____

Contact Name:_____

_____

Telephone 1:_____
Telephone 2:_____

Mobile phone 1:_____
Mobile phone 2:_____

Fax:_____

E-mail 1:_____

_____

E-mail 2:_____

_____

Address 1:_____

_____

Address 2:_____

_____

How we met:_____

_____

Other details:_____

_____

_____

_____

Contact Name: _____

_____

Telephone 1: _____
Telephone 2: _____

Mobile phone 1: _____
Mobile phone 2: _____

Fax: _____

E-mail 1: _____

_____

E-mail 2: _____

_____

Address 1: _____

_____

Address 2: _____

_____

How we met: _____

_____

Other details: _____

_____

_____

_____

Contact Name: _____

_____

Telephone 1: _____
Telephone 2: _____

Mobile phone 1: _____
Mobile phone 2: _____

Fax: _____

E-mail 1: _____

_____

E-mail 2: _____

_____

Address 1: _____

_____

_____

Address 2: _____

_____

How we met: _____

_____

_____

Other details: _____

_____

_____

_____

Contact Name:_____

_____

Telephone 1:_____
Telephone 2:_____

Mobile phone 1:_____
Mobile phone 2:_____

Fax:_____

E-mail 1:_____

_____
E-mail 2:_____

_____

Address 1:_____

_____
Address 2:_____

_____

How we met:_____

_____
Other details:_____

_____
_____
_____

Contact Name: _____

_____

Telephone 1: _____
Telephone 2: _____

Mobile phone 1: _____
Mobile phone 2: _____

Fax: _____

E-mail 1: _____

_____

E-mail 2: _____

_____

Address 1: _____

_____

Address 2: _____

_____

How we met: _____

_____

Other details: _____

_____

_____

_____

Contact Name:_____

_____

Telephone 1:_____
Telephone 2:_____

Mobile phone 1:_____
Mobile phone 2:_____

Fax:_____

E-mail 1:_____

E-mail 2:_____

_____

Address 1:_____

_____

Address 2:_____

_____

How we met:_____

_____

Other details:_____

_____

_____

Contact Name:_____

_____

Telephone 1:_____
Telephone 2:_____

Mobile phone 1:_____
Mobile phone 2:_____

Fax:_____

E-mail 1:_____

_____

E-mail 2:_____

_____

Address 1:_____

_____

Address 2:_____

_____

How we met:_____

_____

Other details:_____

_____

_____

_____

Contact Name: _____

_____

Telephone 1: _____
Telephone 2: _____

Mobile phone 1: _____
Mobile phone 2: _____

Fax: _____

E-mail 1: _____

_____
E-mail 2: _____

_____

Address 1: _____

_____

_____
Address 2: _____

_____

How we met: _____

_____

_____
Other details: _____

_____

_____

_____

Contact Name: _____

_____

Telephone 1: _____
Telephone 2: _____

Mobile phone 1: _____
Mobile phone 2: _____

Fax: _____

E-mail 1: _____

_____
E-mail 2: _____

_____

Address 1: _____

_____

_____
Address 2: _____

_____

How we met: _____

_____

_____
Other details: _____

_____

_____

_____

Contact Name:_____

_____

Telephone 1:_____
Telephone 2:_____

Mobile phone 1:_____
Mobile phone 2:_____

Fax:_____

E-mail 1:_____
_____
E-mail 2:_____
_____

Address 1:_____
_____
_____
Address 2:_____
_____

How we met:_____
_____
_____
Other details:_____
_____
_____
_____

Contact Name: _____

_____

Telephone 1: _____
Telephone 2: _____

Mobile phone 1: _____
Mobile phone 2: _____

Fax: _____

E-mail 1: _____

_____
E-mail 2: _____

_____

Address 1: _____

_____
Address 2: _____

_____

How we met: _____

_____
Other details: _____

_____
_____
_____

Contact Name:_____

_____

Telephone 1:_____
Telephone 2:_____

Mobile phone 1:_____
Mobile phone 2:_____

Fax:_____

E-mail 1:_____
_____
E-mail 2:_____
_____

Address 1:_____
_____
Address 2:_____
_____

How we met:_____
_____
Other details:_____
_____
_____
_____

Contact Name:_____

_____

Telephone 1:_____
Telephone 2:_____

Mobile phone 1:_____
Mobile phone 2:_____

Fax:_____

E-mail 1:_____

_____

E-mail 2:_____

_____

Address 1:_____

_____

Address 2:_____

_____

How we met:_____

_____

Other details:_____

_____

_____

_____

Contact Name:_____

_____

Telephone 1:_____
Telephone 2:_____

Mobile phone 1:_____
Mobile phone 2:_____

Fax:_____

E-mail 1:_____

_____

E-mail 2:_____

_____

Address 1:_____

_____

Address 2:_____

_____

How we met:_____

_____

Other details:_____

_____

_____

_____

Contact Name:_____

_____

Telephone 1:_____
Telephone 2:_____

Mobile phone 1:_____
Mobile phone 2:_____

Fax:_____

E-mail 1:_____
_____
E-mail 2:_____
_____

Address 1:_____
_____
_____
Address 2:_____
_____

How we met:_____
_____
_____
Other details:_____
_____
_____
_____

Contact Name:_____

_____

Telephone 1:_____
Telephone 2:_____

Mobile phone 1:_____
Mobile phone 2:_____

Fax:_____

E-mail 1:_____

_____
E-mail 2:_____

_____

Address 1:_____

_____
_____
Address 2:_____

_____

How we met:_____

_____
_____
Other details:_____

_____
_____
_____

Contact Name: _____

_____

Telephone 1: _____
Telephone 2: _____

Mobile phone 1: _____
Mobile phone 2: _____

Fax: _____

E-mail 1: _____

_____

E-mail 2: _____

_____

Address 1: _____

_____

_____

Address 2: _____

_____

How we met: _____

_____

_____

Other details: _____

_____

_____

_____

Contact Name: _____

_____

Telephone 1: _____
Telephone 2: _____

Mobile phone 1: _____
Mobile phone 2: _____

Fax: _____

E-mail 1: _____

E-mail 2: _____

_____

Address 1: _____

_____

Address 2: _____

_____

How we met: _____

_____

Other details: _____

_____

_____

_____

Contact Name:_____

_____

Telephone 1:_____
Telephone 2:_____

Mobile phone 1:_____
Mobile phone 2:_____

Fax:_____

E-mail 1:_____

_____

E-mail 2:_____

_____

Address 1:_____

_____

Address 2:_____

_____

How we met:_____

_____

Other details:_____

_____

_____

_____

Contact Name: _____

_____

Telephone 1: _____
Telephone 2: _____

Mobile phone 1: _____
Mobile phone 2: _____

Fax: _____

E-mail 1: _____

E-mail 2: _____

Address 1: _____

Address 2: _____

How we met: _____

Other details: _____

Contact Name:_____

_____

Telephone 1:_____
Telephone 2:_____

Mobile phone 1:_____
Mobile phone 2:_____

Fax:_____

E-mail 1:_____

_____

E-mail 2:_____

_____

Address 1:_____

_____

_____

Address 2:_____

_____

How we met:_____

_____

_____

Other details:_____

_____

_____

_____

Contact Name: _____

_____

Telephone 1:_____
Telephone 2:_____

Mobile phone 1:_____
Mobile phone 2:_____

Fax:_____

E-mail 1:_____
_____
E-mail 2:_____
_____

Address 1:_____
_____
Address 2:_____
_____

How we met:_____
_____
Other details:_____
_____
_____
_____

Contact Name: _____

_____

Telephone 1: _____

Telephone 2: _____

Mobile phone 1: _____

Mobile phone 2: _____

Fax: _____

E-mail 1: _____

_____

E-mail 2: _____

_____

Address 1: _____

_____

_____

Address 2: _____

_____

How we met: _____

_____

_____

Other details: _____

_____

_____

_____

Contact Name:_____

_____

Telephone 1:_____
Telephone 2:_____

Mobile phone 1:_____
Mobile phone 2:_____

Fax:_____

E-mail 1:_____

_____
E-mail 2:_____

_____

Address 1:_____

_____

_____
Address 2:_____

_____

How we met:_____

_____

_____
Other details:_____

_____

_____

_____

Contact Name: _____

_____

Telephone 1: _____

Telephone 2: _____

Mobile phone 1: _____

Mobile phone 2: _____

Fax: _____

E-mail 1: _____

_____

E-mail 2: _____

_____

Address 1: _____

_____

_____

Address 2: _____

_____

How we met: _____

_____

_____

Other details: _____

_____

_____

_____

Contact Name: _____

_____

Telephone 1: _____
Telephone 2: _____

Mobile phone 1: _____
Mobile phone 2: _____

Fax: _____

E-mail 1: _____

_____

E-mail 2: _____

_____

Address 1: _____

_____

_____

Address 2: _____

_____

How we met: _____

_____

_____

Other details: _____

_____

_____

_____

Contact Name: _____

_____

Telephone 1: _____
Telephone 2: _____

Mobile phone 1: _____
Mobile phone 2: _____

Fax: _____

E-mail 1: _____

_____

E-mail 2: _____

_____

Address 1: _____

_____

_____

Address 2: _____

_____

How we met: _____

_____

_____

Other details: _____

_____

_____

_____

Contact Name: _____

_____

Telephone 1: _____
Telephone 2: _____

Mobile phone 1: _____
Mobile phone 2: _____

Fax: _____

E-mail 1: _____

_____
E-mail 2: _____

_____

Address 1: _____

_____

Address 2: _____

_____

How we met: _____

_____

Other details: _____

_____

_____

_____

Contact Name: _____

_____

Telephone 1: _____
Telephone 2: _____

Mobile phone 1: _____
Mobile phone 2: _____

Fax: _____

E-mail 1: _____

_____
E-mail 2: _____

_____

Address 1: _____

_____
Address 2: _____

_____

How we met: _____

_____
Other details: _____

_____

_____

_____

Contact Name: _____

_____

Telephone 1: _____
Telephone 2: _____

Mobile phone 1: _____
Mobile phone 2: _____

Fax: _____

E-mail 1: _____

E-mail 2: _____

Address 1: _____

Address 2: _____

How we met: _____

Other details: _____

_____

_____

Contact Name:_____

_____

Telephone 1:_____
Telephone 2:_____

Mobile phone 1:_____
Mobile phone 2:_____

Fax:_____

E-mail 1:_____

_____

E-mail 2:_____

_____

Address 1:_____

_____

_____

Address 2:_____

_____

How we met:_____

_____

_____

Other details:_____

_____

_____

_____

Contact Name:_____

_____

Telephone 1:_____
Telephone 2:_____

Mobile phone 1:_____
Mobile phone 2:_____

Fax:_____

E-mail 1:_____

E-mail 2:_____

Address 1:_____

Address 2:_____

How we met:_____

Other details:_____

_____

_____

Contact Name:_____

_____

Telephone 1:_____
Telephone 2:_____

Mobile phone 1:_____
Mobile phone 2:_____

Fax:_____

E-mail 1:_____

_____

E-mail 2:_____

_____

Address 1:_____

_____

_____

Address 2:_____

_____

How we met:_____

_____

_____

Other details:_____

_____

_____

_____

Contact Name:_____

_____

Telephone 1:_____
Telephone 2:_____

Mobile phone 1:_____
Mobile phone 2:_____

Fax:_____

E-mail 1:_____
_____
E-mail 2:_____
_____

Address 1:_____
_____
_____
Address 2:_____
_____

How we met:_____
_____
_____
Other details:_____
_____
_____
_____